Harlan County Board of Education
Property of Title I
Purchased with Title I Funds

ANIMAL ODYSSEYS

THE WILDEBEEST'S GREAT MIGRATION

Lynn M. Stone

THE ROURKE CORPORATION, INC.
Vero Beach, FL 32964

Photo Credits:

All photos © Lynn M. Stone.

Library of Congress Cataloging in Publication Data

Stone, Lynn M.
The wildebeest's great migration / by Lynn M. Stone
p. cm. – (Animal odysseys)
Includes index.
Summary: Describes the wildebeest's appearance, behavior, life cycle, migration across the Serengeti grasslands, and future survival.
ISBN 0-86593-103-8
1. Gnus – Tanzania – Serengeti Plain – Juvenile literature. 2. Gnus – Tanzania – Serengeti Plain – Migration – Juvenile literature. [1. Gnus. 2. Serengeti Plain (Tanzania)] I. Title. II. Series: Stone, Lynn M. Animal odysseys.
QL737.U53S744 1991
599.73'58–dc20

90-38384
CIP
AC

CONTENTS

1 THE WILDEBEEST'S GREAT MIGRATION

The Serengeti-Masai Mara grasslands of East Africa are one of the Earth's last great wildlife sanctuaries. Time seems to have stopped here in the border country of Tanzania and Kenya. Spectacular concentrations of animals still gather on these grassy plains just as they did 100 and even 1 million years ago.

Several hundred **species** of birds live in the Serengeti-Mara. Among them are several dozen species of **birds of prey** – vultures, kites, buzzards, and eagles. But even more impressive are the legions of mammals that live in the Serengeti-Mara. Nowhere else on Earth do large mammals live in such a variety and abundance. The grasslands are populated by plant eaters, or **herbivores**, including elephants, zebras, giraffes, black rhinos, and many species of antelope. That army of herbivores is the food base for an unusual abundance of **carnivorous**, or meat-eating, mammals. Three of the

Above: *Nomadic wildebeests are the most plentiful big grazing animals on the Serengeti-Masai Mara grasslands of East Africa.*

world's five "big cats" are there – lions, leopards, cheetahs – along with hyenas, jackals, wild dogs, and several smaller carnivores.

Of all the magnificent large animals, none is more plentiful than the antelope known as wildebeest *(Connochaetes taurinus)*. The wildebeest is also one of the most important of the big plains animals. We'll find out why later in this book.

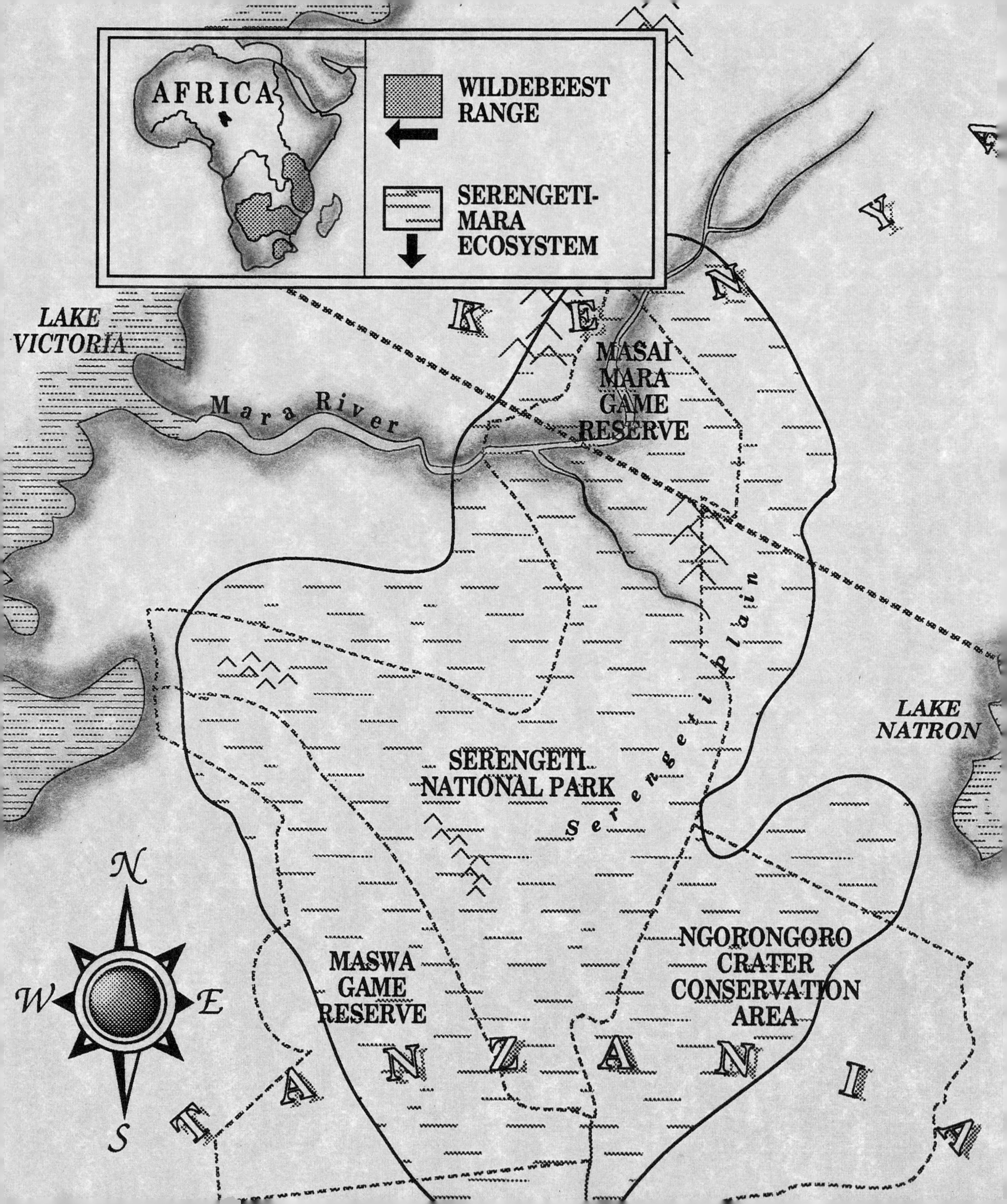
AFRICA
WILDEBEEST RANGE
SERENGETI-MARA ECOSYSTEM
LAKE VICTORIA
KENYA
Mara River
MASAI MARA GAME RESERVE
Serengeti Plain
LAKE NATRON
SERENGETI NATIONAL PARK
MASWA GAME RESERVE
NGORONGORO CRATER CONSERVATION AREA
TANZANIA
N
W
E
S

The wildebeest of the Serengeti are sometimes called brindled gnu (pronounced "new"), blue wildebeest, or white-bearded wildebeest. Whichever label is used, the wildebeest isn't a very handsome creature. (Early Dutch settlers in Africa called the animal a wildebeest because it reminded them of a wild ox, *bees* in their language.) But the huge herds of wildebeests that thunder across the Serengeti and Mara plains are an awesome spectacle. Nowhere is there a **migration** of herd animals on the scale of theirs.

Left: *Migratory range of wildebeests in the Serengeti ecosystem.*

Not all wildebeests are migratory. That is, not all of them make a regular seasonal journey from one location to another. Most of the wildebeest in the Serengeti-Mara region, however, do migrate. Their seasonal wanderings are known in East Africa simply as "the migration."

Today the wildebeest herd in the Serengeti-Mara numbers about 1.3 million. Even the hundreds of thousands of migratory kob antelope in Africa's Sudan and the caribou herds in North America can't compare in size. Nowhere on the planet is there anything quite like the wildebeests' great migration.

2 THE CURIOUS WILDEBEEST

The grayish-brown wildebeest grazing on the Serengeti plains doesn't look exactly like a dairy cow or ox, but there is some similarity. Wildebeests, like cattle, antelope, bison, buffalo, goats, and sheep, belong to the family of mammals called **bovids**. Bovids are plant-eating animals with hooves and four-chambered stomachs. Most of them have a gallbladder, one of the internal organs they share with humans. All male bovids have hollow horns, and most female bovids have horns, too.

Right: *Wildebeests lack the gracefulness and long slender horns typical of many antelope.*

Bovids chew a **cud**. In that respect certainly, the wildebeest is very much like an ordinary dairy cow. The cud is food which has been swallowed but not digested. A wildebeest brings up food – the cud – from the first compartment of its stomach into its mouth. At its leisure, the animal chews the food and swallows it again. This time the food is thoroughly digested as it passes through the animal's stomach chambers.

Wildebeests are one of the bovids called antelope, although they lack the gracefulness and long, slender horns typical of many antelope. Instead, the wildebeest looks as though it had been built from nature's scraps. The body could have been a cow's. The black mane must have been borrowed from a horse. The short, upcurved horns are bison-like. The drapes of long, dark hair on the shoulders and neck could have been from a musk ox.

The wildebeest has a large head and muzzle. Its tail is anchored by a tassel of hair that drops to the animal's heel. The legs are spindly, too slender, it seems, to reckon with carrying a 300- to 600-pound animal.

The wildebeest only looks like nature's mistake. In fact, it is far from that. The wildebeest has been part of the Serengeti for at least 1 million years. Had it been a "mistake," less suited to its **environment**, or surroundings, the wildebeest would have vanished thousands of years ago as many species of mammals did.

No, the wildebeest is not an error in nature's plan. Despite its curious appearance and equally curious habits, it is wonderfully suited, or **adapted**, to its environment. To detect **predators**, the animals that hunt it, the wildebeest has excellent vision, sense of smell, and hearing. Its long legs and hooves are ideal for running on the open plains. If necessary, the wildebeest can last from three to five days without water in its sometimes-parched world.

A wildebeest spends much of its day – indeed, much of its life – on the move. Traveling is a way of life for the Serengeti wildebeest. As a herd gobbles up grass in one area, it continually moves toward another, greener pasture.

Wildebeests have to be able to travel with the herd almost from the moment they are born. A wildebeest calf can stand five minutes after birth. Within a week it can gallop up to 30 miles per hour. To help improve its chance of survival, a wildebeest calf is usually born at mid-day. Lions, dogs, and hyenas are less likely then to be on the prowl.

About 80 percent of wildebeest calves are born between late January and mid-March. Having thousands of calves within just a few weeks works to the advantage of the wildebeest. The Serengeti wildebeest has many predators – big cats, wild dogs, and hyenas. There are far more calves, however, than the predators can kill and eat. Soon, the surviving calves are too big and fast to be easy **prey**. For predators, the birth of thousands of wildebeest within weeks is like having breakfast, lunch, and dinner all at once. There is just too much to eat. If the calves were born throughout the year, predators would be able to take a much greater percentage of them.

Throughout its entire life, a wildebeest is potential prey for large predators. But a calf leads a particu-

larly dangerous existence. If it escapes predators, it still has to contend with disease and with losing its mother and her milk. A calf may have no trouble staying with the herd, but staying in touch with its mother can be a mountain of a problem. Wildebeest herds are often com-

Above: *Lions kill a wildebeest by gaining a stranglehold on the animal's neck.*

posed of thousands of animals. When they bolt from predators or cross rivers, the herds become disorganized. Slower animals are left behind.

Below: *Wildebeest calves stay with their mothers for about one year.*

A calf separated from its mother will wander through the herd and bleat in an attempt to find her. Scientists believe that a cow may be able to recognize her calf's bleating as well as its smell. But the likelihood of

the calf locating its mother is small. Unfortunately for an orphan calf, a wildebeest cow other than its real mother will not let it nurse and tag along.

A young wildebeest lives with its mother for about a year. Young bulls form bachelor herds until, at three or four years of age, they are old enough to fight for cows and mate. Actually, wildebeest "fights" are rarely more than staged displays, like professional wrestling. These mock battles occur during the **rut**, or mating season. Wildebeest bulls shed their mild manners during the rut, which usually peaks in June. They stomp, snort, kick, grunt, and generally act ugly toward each other. Each bull tries to defend a territory that is no more than a small patch of ground. "Fights" are waged over rights to the females. A bull tries to corner as many cows as it can on its piece of the Serengeti.

A fight begins when two bulls charge each other. As the gap between them closes, they drop to their knees and face each other. They may touch horns or push, but usually they make no physical contact whatsoever.

Bulls have a hard time keeping cows with them. Always restless, wildebeest cows tend to move from one bull's territory to another's. During the rut, a cow may mate with several bulls.

A female wildebeest sometimes mates at just 15 months of age. Usually the cow is two years old. A cow normally calves each year until she is at least 12. Wildebeests can live to be 18 years old.

Restlessness and a **nomadic** lifestyle are basic to being a wildebeest. There are three bands of wildebeests in the Serengeti-Mara **ecosystem**, however, that are not part of a grand migration. They travel comparatively short distances. These particular herds find grass and water year-round within fairly confined areas. Beyond the Serengeti-Mara ecosystem, wildebeests are found in lesser numbers in southern Africa, southwestern Africa, and in other parts of eastern Africa.

Throughout their range, wildebeests have experienced **cycles** in their population. Some animal populations remain fairly constant or show gradual gains and losses. Wildebeest populations, in contrast, have risen and fallen drastically because of disease, drought, and changes in the amount of grassland available to them. In recent years, the Serengeti-Mara population has risen sharply. A key reason for that is the disappearance of rinderpest, a measleslike virus that wiped out large numbers of wildebeests, buffalo, and giraffes about 100 years ago. Now that domestic animals are inoculated against the disease, which was brought to Africa from Europe, the virus has been controlled.

3 WILDEBEEST COUNTRY

More than anything else, the Serengeti-Mara region is a rolling plain carpeted by grass. Here and there are acacia trees, singly and in greater numbers in the grassy, open woodlands called **savannas**. The flow of grass on the plains is interrupted by rocky

Left: *The Serengeti-Mara region includes grassy, open woodlands called savannas.*

Above: *Columns of wildebeests travel over African grassland that looks much like the North American prairie.*

outcrops known as kopjes and by rivers and their ribbons of lush forest. But the Serengeti-Mara is essentially grassland, 10,000 square miles of it.

This part of Africa is not the jungle that you may imagine Africa to be. In general appearance, it resembles the grasslands, or prairies, of midwestern and western North America. It's difficult now to imagine the once-sprawling American prairie. Most of the prairie was plowed and planted in corn, beans, and grain. The last

Above:
A thunderstorm rumbles over the herds of wildebeests and Burchell's zebras.

herds of free-roaming bison were destroyed in the late 1800s. Even 200 years ago, however, the variety of wildlife on the American prairies did not compare with that of the Serengeti-Mara grasslands today.

The Serengeti-Mara plains are wildebeest country. Here wildebeests, along with thousands of other animals, live in concert with the climate and their surroundings. The animals have relationships with each other and with the land. Together in a natural community, the Serengeti-Mara ecosystem, the animals and plants form a great web of interactions, or relationships. **Ecologists**, the scientists who study the relationships between plants and animals, call these relationships the **food web**. Through the food web, energy passes from plants to animals and, ultimately, back into the environment. You will read more about the wildebeest's role in the food web in the chapter on predators and prey.

For the animals of the Serengeti-Mara, the seasons are marked by changes in rainfall rather than by temperature and length of daylight. Along the Earth's equator, air temperatures in any one location remain quite constant. In this part of equatorial Africa, days range from warm to hot, and nights are cool. But rainfall varies considerably. Both a wet season and a dry season occur. Rain, or the lack of it, naturally has a huge influence on the growth of grass and, therefore, on the animals that consume it.

The rainy season begins and ends with black thunder clouds piling up over the plains. The entire Serengeti doesn't turn green from these spotty early and late storms, but some part of the plains does. Wherever that happens to be, the area with the rainfall becomes a magnet for wildebeests.

Much of the territory where the wildebeests live has been protected from hunting and development by the governments of Kenya and Tanzania. Serengeti National Park lies wholly within northern Tanzania. The much smaller Masai Mara National Reserve – named in part for the Masai tribe which lives in this region – is in Kenya. The Mara reserve is the northern extension of the Serengeti ecosystem.

The Mara is the wettest part of the ecosystem. On the average, 53 inches of rain fall there each year, with the heaviest rains in December, January, and April. Having been fed with more moisture, Mara grasses are taller than those on the Serengeti. When the short grasses on the Serengeti dry up, wildebeests can still find plenty of fresh grass in the Mara region.

Grass, of course, is the essence of wildebeest country and the staff of life for these animals. If it weren't for the oceans of grass, there would be no wildebeests on the plains. The grasses themselves are the products of several factors, chief among them being the soil.

The Serengeti is covered by powdery volcanic soil under which is extremely hard ground. Grass can grow almost anywhere, and the Serengeti is ideal for it. Trees find it difficult to root in the hard ground, and they have a hard time competing with the grass roots, which are already established. Elephants and grazing animals discourage the growth of trees on the plains, too. Animals may eat, trample, or uproot little trees. Prolonged drought is much more destructive to trees than grass; likewise, fires destroy little trees while not harming the roots of grass plants.

Grasses of many species live in the Serengeti-Mara ecosystem. The shorter grasses live in areas of the least rainfall. Especially in the southeastern part of the Serengeti, the grass lies in the rain shadow of the Crater Highlands. Like mountains anywhere, the Crater Highlands intercept moisture which might otherwise fall on the plains. Only about 22 inches of rain fall in the southeastern Serengeti compared with the 50-plus inches in the northern sector. As you would expect, taller grasses grow in this area.

The grass, clearly, is essential for the wildebeest. But wildebeests are also of some benefit to the grass. By their presence, huge numbers of wildebeests have probably helped prevent the spread of acacia trees and thickets of croton into the grassland. And ecologists have shown that the grazing of wildebeests on the short-grass Serengeti plains stimulates the growth of more grass. Grazing also creates a greater variety of the low-growing grasses that wildebeest like.

4 THE REMARKABLE JOURNEY

At a distance, they could be an army of ants as they file over low, yellow hills and onto the plains above the Mara River. Across the plains, as far as anyone can see, are the black strings of wildebeest–running, grazing, always moving closer to the Mara. Knots of zebras and the plains-colored Thompson's gazelles are scattered among the wildebeest herds. At times, the grassland itself seems to be in motion with the herds.

Late on an August morning, a few zebras and a herd of wildebeests reach a clearing on a bank several feet above the brown, rushing Mara River. The open plains end abruptly here in a clutter of thickets that wind with the river. A broad gap in the bush, however, allows the animals clear passage down a muddy embankment to the river's edge. It is a path that wildebeests have probably used for generations. The first animals to reach the low bluff above the river are nervous. They snort, paw at the earth, and kick up spirals of

Above: *River crossings are dangerous, frantic times for migrating wildebeest herds.*

dust. The animals at the bluff's edge look across the Mara. Beyond a screen of thickets, the rolling plains on the other side are a patchwork of yellow grass and clumps of brush. Wildebeests and zebras are already there, fanning across the rises and gullies.

Whatever attraction the animals on the far side may be to the gathering herd, it is not quite enough to provoke these new arrivals to join them. A dozen zebras anxiously gallop away from the river and wander back in the direction they came from. The instinct to move ahead is powerful, but so, too, is the instinct to turn and run

Above:
In a show of determination and grit, swimming wildebeests battle the swift current of the Mara River.

from this new challenge. Meanwhile, more and more animals, most of them wildebeests, bunch up on the clearing by the river. Farther away the oncoming herds begin to move more urgently, as if they are missing something. The excitement in the herds grows.

Finally, and suddenly, something does happen. There is no horn, bell, or signal of any kind. A small herd of zebras scrambles down the muddy bank and plunges into the river. Upriver from the crossing, hippos splash and blow water vapor through their nostrils. They ignore the swimming zebras and the hundreds of wildebeests poised to invade their river retreat.

The current in the Mara River has quite a kick this day, and it pushes the zebras downstream. But the zebras are strong, confident swimmers. On the run, they splash from the river on the opposite bank some distance downstream from their plunge. The zebras clamber up a slope of grass and dirt and bound onto the plains on the far shore.

Below:
A wildebeest that avoided rocks, crocodiles, and drowning splashes ashore after fording the Mara River.

The zebra crossing seems to energize the wildebeests. No sooner have the zebras crossed the Mara than the wildebeests, gathered now into a grunting and bellowing black mass, begin their crossing. The first wildebeests hurtle crazily into the Mara. They are followed by

Above: *Wildebeests run blindly into a muddy ravine that leads nowhere after they have crossed the river.*

dozens more. The dark bodies almost disappear in the river. Only the wildebeests' heads, their eyes wild with fright, show as they frantically steer for the far shore. What began as an orderly crossing by the zebras has become pandemonium.

The wildebeests slip downstream, caught in the swift surge of the Mara. What they lack in orderliness they make up for with sheer will and grit. Wildebeests begin splashing from the river and dashing up the far bank. Miraculously, in their haste, the swimming wildebeests manage to avoid rocks, and one beast narrowly misses being taken into the jaws of a Nile crocodile. The crocs, which grow to 18 feet in length, fear nothing in the river and eat almost anything. Wildebeests are fair game.

Rocks and crocodiles are not the only hazards of river crossings. As they struggle up the slick river banks, now at several exit points, the animals slam into each other. If one stumbles, the others charge on. Some fall from muddy trails back into the river. Others run blindly into a ravine that leads nowhere. One wildebeest nearly disappears as it's trampled by its companions into the mud. A calf stands alone on a muddy shelf. The crossing and the confusion go on. Hundreds of wildebeests, driven forward by the urge to follow, crash into the Mara, swim

Below:
A vulture descends onto a logjam of drowned wildebeests.

furiously to buck the current, and find whatever passage they can to the plains. For a few minutes, both shores are full of wildebeest. Then, like a faucet being turned off, it's over. This herd's crossing has ended, and most of them have made it. There are deeper pools, steeper banks than these.

For some, however, the crossing ends in exhaustion, broken legs, or drowning. Rest may remedy the exhaustion. The wildebeest with broken legs will surely be killed by predators. The drowned animals will be hurried by the current downstream to stack against fallen trees. Vultures will discover them and gorge themselves.

The great migration of the wildebeests neither begins nor ends with a river crossing. In fact, the migration doesn't really begin or end at all. For the wildebeest, migration – wandering, at least – is an ongoing process. River crossings are just one of the hurdles in the process.

Most animals that we associate with migration, such as geese and wild swans, make a predictable, seasonal journey of some distance. Then they remain at their summer or winter home for a fairly long time, perhaps five months. These migrations have a rather precise beginning and end. Wildebeest, on the other hand, are forever milling about, even when they reach a distant point of their travels.

Most of the Serengeti-Mara wildebeests migrate simply because they cannot obtain enough food and water by staying in one place for the whole year. They usually travel in a predictable direction and over somewhat traditional routes. They don't always travel, however, at precisely the same time or to precisely the same places. Rain has a tremendous influence on where and when they go. If the Serengeti has an unusually wet year, for example, the wildebeests are less likely to migrate in large numbers into the Mara. Even on a day-to-day basis, wildebeests travel with an eye to the rain. Rain, of course, means green grass, but how do wildebeests know that? Scientists think that wildebeests may associate thunder and lightning, which often accompany the scattered rains, with good pasture. Perhaps the animals can smell rain. However the animals process rain clues, they seem to know where to go to find green pasture.

Generally, the wettest part of the year is November through April. The great herds wander through the short grass pastures of the southeast Serengeti at that time. As the rains taper off, the wildebeests move north into the so-called western corridor of the Serengeti in May and June. The grasses are taller there than in the lower Serengeti. As that region dries out, the herds drift north into the open woodlands of the northern Serengeti and the Masai Mara in July. They linger in the north as late as October, then wander south again using a somewhat different route than the one on which they journeyed north. An individual wildebeest in the Serengeti-Mara ecosystem may travel nearly 1,900 miles on its annual migratory route. That averages over 50 miles each day! If it were not for several surrounding physical barriers – Lake Victoria, the Isuria Escarpment, the wooded hills of Loita and Gol, the Crater Highlands, and the Eyasi Escarpment – the migration would be even more widespread.

Wildebeests usually travel in columns. In years when the rainy season ends abruptly, the northward migration involves hundreds of thousands of wildebeests leaving the southern Serengeti at once. Their advancing columns fanned across the plains form one of the most amazing sights in nature.

The wildebeests' great **odyssey** across the plains ensures that the plains will be there for odysseys to follow. Grazing clips the grasses and keeps them growing. Grazing also reduces the chances of harmful fires. By eating the grass, the herd animals remove what otherwise might become kindling for extremely hot, long-burning fires.

Such a colossal herd of animals might be expected to damage the grassland, but it doesn't. The wildebeests aren't in any one area long enough to damage it. They don't uproot grass; they mow it. Meanwhile, their manure enriches the ground and recycles nutrients.

5
PREDATORS AND PREY

In the shade of an acacia tree, a pair of male cheetahs were lounging away the midday. They had tried earlier that morning to kill, but they had not been successful. They had trotted toward the grazing herds to test them. Would the animals easily run off, or would one straggle behind and reveal its weakness? Twice the cheetahs had joined in an effortless trot toward the herds. Twice the herds had stampeded, hooves thundering, dust billowing. And neither time had there been stragglers. Where the herds had been, the plains were empty. For now, the acacia's shade was the best deal the cheetahs were going to get.

Nearly 500 feet from the cheetahs, a wildebeest calf walked unsteadily into the grass. Perhaps five months old, the calf had apparently lost its mother. There were hundreds of wildebeests scattered around the plains, but the calf was quite alone. The wildebeest was thin, and walking was an effort. It stopped and slumped into the grass.

Above: *An orphaned wildebeest calf is easy prey for a pair of cheetahs, the world's fastest land animals.*

Left:
The morning hunt was a failure for the cheetah until a wildebeest calf aroused its attention.

The calf's manner should have stirred the cheetahs. After all, a skinny calf by itself is easy prey. The calf was lucky. The cheetahs' sleepy gaze had been fixed in another direction, and neither of them had seen the calf.

Orphaned wildebeest calves don't survive long on the African savannas. They are singled out by predators. A predator wastes less energy and takes fewer chances if it attacks a sickly animal.

The wildebeest calf was temporarily safe. But a long-legged secretary bird, hunting lizards, stepped near the hiding place. Startled, the wildebeest gathered itself up on rocky legs. This time the calf's movement caught the cheetahs' attention. Instantly they were on their feet and began a quick, deadly march toward the calf.

Despite its weakness, the calf gamely made a final run. It galloped over the dusty plain desperately trying to outdistance the cheetahs. If a cheetah begins its running attack fairly close to its prey, no animal can outrun it. For a hundred yards or so, the cheetah is the fastest land animal in the world, running in excess of 65 miles per hour.

The calf's burst of energy triggered a chase response in the cheetahs. Their easy lope suddenly became

Below: *Wildebeests killed during the migration nourish such scavengers as hyenas, jackals, and the vultures and marabou stork shown here.*

Right:
After just a few days, nothing except a skull is left of a wildebeest killed during the migration.

a tawny blur. In seconds, closing from two sides, they reached the calf. One cat bowled the calf down in a swirl of dust and locked its jaws on the wildebeest's throat. The kill was quick and nearly bloodless.

Left: *Hyenas have exceptionally strong jaws for chewing bones that they tear from carcasses.*

Once again the wildebeest had played an important role in the health of the ecosystem. One wildebeest was gone, but not wasted. Some of the energy stored in the wildebeest would now pass on to the cats. When the cheetahs had finished eating, or were driven off the kill by lions, the wildebeest would eventually feed marabou storks, hyenas, jackals, vultures, insects, and **microorganisms**. After just a few days, the calf would be reduced to a bleached skeleton.

Above:
Wild dogs are the most endangered predators in the Serengeti-Mara ecosystem.

Predation, the killing of one animal by another for food, is essential for the well-being of the ecosystem. It is one of the ways in which animals obtain the food energy they need to live.

All living things need food. Not all of them, of course, have to kill for it. Wildebeests and other herbivores take energy from the plants they consume. The plants, in turn, are nourished by rain, sunlight, and soil. In each case, energy is transferred from one living thing to another.

Because they outnumber the other large herbivores, wildebeests are a vital part of the plant and animal food web in the Serengeti-Mara. Wildebeests are hunted by hyenas, lions, leopards, wild dogs, and cheetahs. More animals feed on them when the predators have eaten their fill.

Hyenas are **scavengers**; they love to gnaw on the **carcasses** of animals killed by lions and other preda-

Below: *Lions feed on wildebeests whenever they are available.*

Above: *Lions share their wildebeest kill with the entire family group, called a pride.*

tors. They are also skillful predators themselves, often hunting in packs called **clans**. Hyenas usually hunt in darkness, their eerie howls and whoops making wild music in the African night.

Hyenas can't sprint with the speed of cheetahs, and they don't ambush prey as leopards and lions sometimes do. However, hyenas are fast and they have the endurance to run long distances. A pack of hyenas can bring down and kill a wildebeest bull.

Wild dogs are the most **endangered** predators in the entire Serengeti-Mara. Probably fewer than a hundred dogs live in the two parks, so they make no real impact on the huge herds of wildebeests.

African wild dogs hunt in packs. They are fast and well-organized. Wild dogs have a much higher success rate than most predators; they usually catch whatever animal they chase.

Unlike the free-roaming hyenas, lions don't normally follow the wildebeest herds very far. But as the migration passes through a lion pride's territory, the big cats regularly attack the wildebeests. Although one cat, usually a lioness, makes the kill, an entire pride may feed on it.

Wildebeests are not alone on their journey, nor in their role as prey for the predators. Some 200,000 Burchell's zebras follow a migratory route similar to the wildebeest's. Another traveler is Thompson's gazelle, a small, swift antelope. Thousands of Thompson's gazelles, or Tommies, journey with the wildebeests during part of the migration.

Zebras and gazelles, like wildebeests, are prey for large carnivores. Cheetahs and wild dogs are often dependent on gazelles. Zebras are a favorite prey of lions.

Wildebeests share the grassland and savanna with several other plant-eating animals – elephants, Grant's

Right:
The African buffalo, accompanied by an oxpecker bird, shares the East African grassland with the wildebeest and other herbivores.

gazelles, Coke's hartebeests, impalas, topis, African buffalo, giraffes, and others. Each species exists comfortably with the others. None has anything to fear from the others, and they don't usually compete for the same foods. A zebra's teeth and mouth, for example, enable it to clip long stems and seed heads from the tall grasses. Wildebeests have broad mouths and lips, better adapted for grazing on leafy, short grasses. Topis have small,

narrow mouths, suited for snipping leaves that might be hidden among long grass stems.

In the Serengeti-Mara ecosystem, each animal has its place, or **niche**. The niche of one species will always be somewhat different from the niches of other species. In that way, each variation of **habitat** within the Serengeti-Mara can be used by one creature or another.

Above: *Topi antelope live on the grasslands with wildebeests, but each of the big grazing animals has a different niche.*

6 FUTURE MIGRATIONS

In the last 35 years, conditions in the Serengeti have been helpful to the wildebeest. First, more grassland became available because of fires that burned off some of the open woodland. Later, the rinderpest virus was fought and controlled. Then, in the 1970s, East Africa experienced greater than usual rainfall during the dry season. The rain produced new grass and gave the grazing animals another source of dry-season food.

With the changing conditions came a surge in the wildebeest population. In 1958, ecologist Bernard Grzimek estimated the total wildebeest population in the Serengeti at about 100,000 animals. Three years later the first census by plane revealed 263,362 wildebeests. In recent years the count has topped 1.3 million.

Wildebeests are thriving now, but is their future secure? No.

One problem that will haunt the wildebeest and other animals is space. A wildebeest's wandering does not take place entirely in the Serengeti or Mara. As the human populations of Tanzania and Kenya grow, conflicts between the interests of people and wildebeests will increase. Wildebeests compete with cattle for grass and water. Already, in the parks and beyond their borders, it is estimated that as many as 50,000 wildebeests are killed by **poachers** each year.

Left: *Wildebeest numbers on the Serengeti-Mara plains have climbed well over 1 million.*

Even the park boundaries are only as secure as the governments of Tanzania and Kenya make them. As long as both countries enjoy stable governments, the park boundaries will be reasonably safe. Both countries want to protect the Serengeti-Mara ecosystem. Not only is it unique among the Earth's natural wonders, but it helps Tanzania and Kenya earn money from tourists.

Meanwhile, scientists continue to study the migration. Tracking the animals with four-wheel drive vehicles and airplanes has already become outdated. Sat-

Above: *Protecting the wildebeests and their land is a goal of the Kenyan and Tanzanian governments and many other people throughout the world.*

ellites can follow wildebeests much more cheaply and efficiently. Among the questions scientists are studying are: How far do individual wildebeest travel in a day? and How much do their migration routes vary? Scientists also want to know if migratory wildebeests sometimes "drop out" and join the smaller, non-migratory herds.

Protecting the great wildebeest migration and the 10,000 square miles of Serengeti and Masai Mara is an enormous and costly job. To do it successfully, it will take more than the good intentions of Tanzania and Kenya. It will take the cooperation of people throughout the world who want to preserve this amazing glimpse of Africa's natural history.

GLOSSARY

adapted – having a characteristic of function, form, or behavior that improves a living thing's chances of survival in its habitat

birds of prey – hunting and scavenging birds – such as hawks, eagles, owls and vultures – distinguished by hooked beaks and talons

bovid – the family of large, hoofed, plant-eating mammals with horns and four-chambered stomachs

carcass – a dead body

carnivorous – meat eating

clan – a group of hyenas

cud – food that has been only partially chewed and digested when brought up from a bovid animal's stomach for more thorough chewing

cycle – a pattern, as in periodic highs and lows in animal populations

ecologist – a scientist who studies the interrelationships of plants and animals in association with their environment

ecosystem – a system of exchanges of food and energy between plants and animals and their environment

endangered – a plant or animal in danger of extinction

environment – the total surroundings in which a plant or animal lives, including soil, water, air, plants and animals

food web – the network of interlocking food chains through which energy passes

habitat – a plant or animal's immediate surroundings; its specific, preferred location within the environment

herbivore – plant-eating animal

microorganism – a microscopic organism invisible to the naked eye

migration – a predictable and seasonal movement from one location to a more distant one

niche – a living thing's role or job in the natural community

nomadic – the characteristic of wandering

odyssey – a long journey

poacher – one who hunts against the law

predation – the preying of one animal on another for food

predator – an animal that kills and feeds on other animals

prey – an animal hunted for food by another animal

rut – the mating season, particularly of horned animals

savanna – an open, grassy woodland

scavenger – an animal that feeds on food scraps left by other animals

species – a group of plants or animals whose members reproduce naturally only with other plants or animals of the same group; a particular kind of plant or animal, such as a *Thompson's* gazelle

INDEX

Numbers in boldface type refer to photo and illustration pages.

WHERE TO SEE WILDEBEESTS

The wildebeests that are the subject of this book live in Tanzania and Kenya, countries in East Africa. Wildebeests live in several other parts of Africa too, but not in the great herds that roam the Serengeti plains ecosystem of northern Tanzania and southern Kenya.

Perhaps the best place in the world to see wildebeests is in Kenya's Masai Mara Game Reserve, the northern extension of the Serengeti ecosystem. Compared to the Serengeti proper, the Masai Mara is small, and it has a permanent population of wildebeest. Visitors never miss seeing these curious, cowlike animals. And during the annual migration, the Mara herd swells into hundreds of thousands.

The migration isn't always predictable, but August and early September are good bets for finding the Masai Mara plains darkened by the wildebeest herds.

Wildebeest Sites

Masai Mara Game Reserve, Kenya
Ngorongoro Crater Conservation Area, Tanzania
Serengeti National Park, Tanzania

Ed. Note: Sites listed here do not represent *all* the places where wildebeest may be observed. They do represent sites that are reliable and have relatively easy access.